KT-593-917

# Indigenous Australian Cultures

Mary Colson

**www.raintreepublishers.co.uk**
Visit our website to find out
more information about
Raintree books.

**To order:**
☎ Phone 0845 6044371
🖷 Fax +44 (0) 1865 312263
🖂 Email myorders@raintreepublishers.co.uk

Customers from outside the UK please telephone +44 1865 312262

Raintree is an imprint of Capstone Global
Library Limited, a company incorporated
in England and Wales having its registered
office at 7 Pilgrim Street, London, EC4V
6LB – Registered company number: 6695582

Text © Capstone Global Library Limited 2013
First published in hardback in 2013
The moral rights of the proprietor have been
asserted.

All rights reserved. No part of this publication
may be reproduced in any form or by any
means (including photocopying or storing
it in any medium by electronic means and
whether or not transiently or incidentally to
some other use of this publication) without
the written permission of the copyright owner,
except in accordance with the provisions
of the Copyright, Designs, and Patents Act
1988 or under the terms of a licence issued
by the Copyright Licensing Agency, Saffron
House, 6–10 Kirby Street, London EC1N
8TS (www.cla.co.uk). Applications for the
copyright owner's written permission should
be addressed to the publisher.

Edited by Charlotte Guillain, Abby Colich,
  and Vaarunika Dharmapala
Designed by Steve Mead
Original illustrations © Capstone Global
  Library Ltd 2013
Illustrations by Oxford Designers & Illustrators
Picture research by Ruth Blair
Originated by Capstone Global Library Ltd
Printed and bound in China by Leo Paper
  Products Ltd

ISBN 978 1 406 24178 5 (hardback)
16 15 14 13 12
10 9 8 7 6 5 4 3 2 1

British Library Cataloguing in Publication Data
Colson, Mary.
Indigenous Australian cultures. -- (Global
cultures)
306'.0899915-dc23
A full catalogue record for this book is
available from the British Library.

Acknowledgements
We would like to thank the following for
permission to reproduce photographs:
Alamy pp. 6 (© Bill Bachman), 7 (© William
Robinson), 11, 23, 26, 38 (© Penny Tweedie),
12 (© Paul Dymond), 14 (© Christine Osborne
Pictures), 20 (© Hemis), 24 (© Danita
Delimont), 27 (© Suzy Bennett), 28 (© LOOK
Die Bildagentur der Fotografen GmbH), 41 (©
David Hancock); Corbis pp. 15 (© Mick Tskias/
X90089/Reuters), 34 (© Reuters), 37 (© STR/
Reuters), 39 (© Oliver Strewe); Getty Images
pp. 5 (David McLain), 8, 16 (Robert Francis/
Robert Harding), 21 (William West/AFP), 29
(Gaye Gerard), 30 (C. Brandon/Redferns),
35 (Glenn Campbell/The Sydney Morning
Herald/Fairfax Media); iStockphoto p. 43
bottom left (© Vito Elefante); Photolibrary p.
10 (Pepeira Tom/Iconotec); Photoshot pp. 9,
18, 25, 33 (Penny Tweedie); Scala, Florence
p. 19 (The Metropolitan Museum of Art/Art
Resource); Rex Features p. 31 (Paul Lovelace);
Shutterstock p. 36 (© Curioso), 43 top (©
EcoPrint), 43 bottom right (© Hocus-Focus),
design features (© trendywest).

Cover photograph of a smiling Indigenous
Australian boy reproduced with permission of
Getty Images (Penny Tweedie). Cover design
feature of a dot painting reproduced with
permission of Shutterstock (© trendywest).

Every effort has been made to contact
copyright holders of any material reproduced
in this book. Any omissions will be rectified
in subsequent printings if notice is given to
the publisher.

Disclaimer
All the internet addresses (URLs) given in this
book were valid at the time of going to press.
However, due to the dynamic nature of the
internet, some addresses may have changed,
or sites may have changed or ceased to exist
since publication. While the author and
publisher regret any inconvenience this may
cause readers, no responsibility for any such
changes can be accepted by either the author
or the publisher.

# CONTENTS

| RENFREWSHIRE COUNCIL | |
| --- | --- |
| 184198321 | |
| Bertrams | 16/01/2013 |
| 306.089 | £13.99 |
| FOX | |

Some words are shown in bold, **like this**. You can find out what they mean by looking in the glossary.

# INTRODUCING INDIGENOUS AUSTRALIAN CULTURES

What do you know about **Indigenous** Australian **cultures**? Have you seen pictures of ancient cave paintings? Do you think of **didgeridoos** and people living in harmony with the land?

## First people

*Aborigine* is a Latin word meaning "from the beginning". The word was used by white settlers to describe the indigenous people of Australia and the Torres Strait Islands, located off the coast of present-day Queensland.

It is believed that Indigenous Australians came to Australia and the Torres Strait Islands 50,000 to 60,000 years ago from South-East Asia. Indigenous Australian people believe they have always lived there, that they were created by spirit **ancestors**. Europeans arrived to settle in Australia in 1788. There have been many problems and conflicts between the two groups of people.

There are 550,000 Indigenous Australians, who make up about 1 per cent of Australia's population. Each different indigenous group or "nation", such as the Eora, Yari-Yarit, and Djidjijamba, has its own language. Some nations have just a few family groups, while others include hundreds of people.

## Did you know?

Indigenous Australian people do not always use the word *Aborigine* to describe themselves. They may also use words such as Koori, Murri, and Nyungar.

## What is culture?

Culture is the values, beliefs, and attitudes of a particular place. It is about how people live and worship, and about the music, art, and literature they produce. Indigenous Australian cultures have developed over thousands of years. This book explores different features of these ancient and peaceful cultures.

Indigenous Australian cultures are some of the oldest continuous cultures in the world.

# BELIEFS AND FESTIVALS

The Dreamtime is what Indigenous Australians call the beginning of the world. Their stories, art, and music explain different parts of the Dreamtime and pass on important beliefs to new generations. Dreamtime stories include why fish swim, and how the landscape was created by different spirit ancestors. Each nation usually has its own spirit and **creation story**. However, some stories are shared, such as the story of Baiame, the creation spirit.

## In the beginning

Most indigenous people believe that in the beginning the world had no mountains, rocks, or rivers. They believe that spirit ancestors came out of the ground and began to shape the landscape as they moved. For example, a mountain may be the fallen body of a spirit ancestor. Indigenous Australians believe that some of these ancestors gave birth to humans. Spirit ancestors can be humans, animals, rocks, trees, or stars. There are ancestral kangaroos and ancestral fish.

This sand painting (see page 15) was made by the Ipolera people of central Australia.

## Did you know?

Indigenous Australians find their way across the country using songlines. They believe the whole country is mapped with the invisible tracks of the spirit ancestors, who sang out the names of everything that crossed their path. By singing the ancestors' songs today, Indigenous Australians can find their way around.

## The Rainbow Serpent

Indigenous Australians believe the Rainbow Serpent wriggled across Australia and created rivers and mountains, the Sun, fire, and all the colours. The Rainbow Serpent's song describes the landscape made by her journey.

Indigenous Australians believe that ancestral beings still live in the mountains, rivers, and waterholes that they created.

## Spirit ancestors

Each Indigenous Australian nation believes in different spirit ancestors. Each person has their own individual spirit ancestor that they believe they came from and are connected to. Indigenous Australians believe that most of the spirit ancestors are good. However, there are also some very nasty ones.

## Did you know?

Indigenous Australian nations near Laura in Queensland believe the Anurra spirit can bounce 0.8 kilometres (half a mile) in one hop. It is believed the Anurra lives on frogs and has large ears.

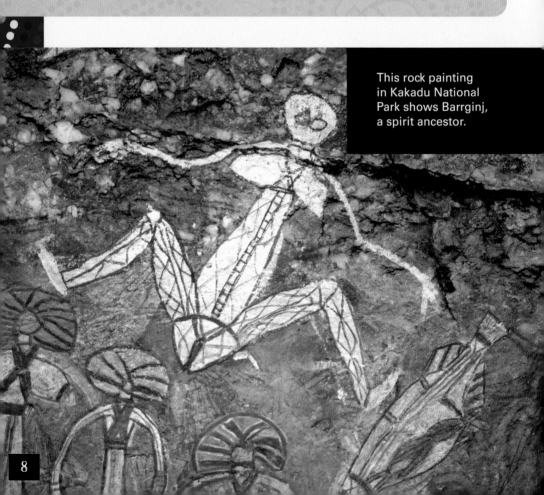

This rock painting in Kakadu National Park shows Barrginj, a spirit ancestor.

Indigenous Australians believe a giant serpent guards waterholes like this one.

## The Quinkan

The Quinkan spirit is believed to live in the rocks near Jowalbinna in Queensland. The Quinkan has two parts to his being: one good, one bad. The bad Quinkan is big, fat, and scary, and does all kinds of mischief. To keep the Quinkan happy, Indigenous Australians believe he should not be disturbed, so there are Quinkan reserves and areas that only indigenous people can enter.

## Did you know?

The *bunyip* is a fearsome creature that is believed to lurk in ponds and streams. Most indigenous nations consider it an evil spirit and have different names for it, such as *dongu* and *wowee-wowee*. The word *bunyip* has entered general Australian English and means "imposter" (someone who does not belong in a place).

## Sacred sites and ceremonies

Each Indigenous Australian nation has its own sacred sites. These are the places where it is believed the spirit ancestors came out of the ground and where they still live.

Ceremonies are at the heart of Indigenous Australian **heritage**. This is the way people have always kept in touch with spirit ancestors. Birth, marriage, and death are all marked with special ceremonies. At funerals, a smoking ceremony is performed. Special plants are burned to create a purifying smoke. Indigenous Australians believe this will heal the sadness. When someone dies, family members call out to the spirit ancestors to make sure that a person's spirit will rejoin the spirit world.

Uluru is a sacred site for the Pitjantjatjara and the Yankunytjatjara peoples. Visitors are asked not to walk on the rock out of respect for the spirit ancestors.

## YOUNG PEOPLE

A *bora* is an **initiation** ceremony in which teenage boys become men. Beforehand, boys learn songs, stories, dances, and traditional **folklore**. For the ceremony, the boys, known as *kippas*, decorate themselves with paint. A *bora* is still an important **rite of passage** for Indigenous Australian teenagers.

### Tjurunga

For nations such as the Arrernte, *tjurunga* (also known as *churinga*) are important religious objects and songs. *Tjurunga* might be sacred earth mounds where ceremonies take place, or stone or wooden objects. In Arrernte ceremonies, special religious paintings are made on the ground and sacred songs are sung.

This is an image of an initiation ceremony from the film *Yolngu Boy* (2001). The film tells the story of three Indigenous Australian boys, who are able to combine their **traditions** with modern Australian life.

## Festivals and traditions

All over Australia, there are festivals to celebrate Indigenous Australian cultures. These festivals keep indigenous cultures alive and developing for the next generation. Everybody is welcome and crafts, music, and dance are on show.

## Cultural celebration

The Garma Festival in Arnhem Land is one of north Australia's most important indigenous festivals. Nation groups from all over Arnhem Land and the Northern Territory attend. Garma is a celebration of cultural traditions and practices including dance, song, music, and art.

The Indigenous Australian Dance Festival at Laura in Queensland is held at the site of a very old *bora* ground.

The Garma festival is also a conference where speakers discuss Indigenous Australian issues and concerns. They debate how to improve life for Indigenous Australians, and try to get the government to listen to their ideas.

Passing on knowledge to the next generation is a central part of Indigenous Australian culture. This helps to make sure that ancient traditions survive, in spite of all the changes that have happened since Europeans settled the country. Young people learn their nation's stories, knowledge, and wisdom by listening to their **elders**.

## YOUNG PEOPLE

Young Indigenous Australians of the Yolngu nation in Arnhem Land learn about their culture through a process called *madayin*. This is when the knowledge of how to live life well is given from one elder to a younger person. There are "owners" or "holders" of various types of knowledge. All young Yolngu seek knowledge from different people who are experts. As the young people get older, they in turn become "owners" of certain knowledge, which they then pass on to the next generation.

## Did you know?

There are many Indigenous Australian groups that travel the country giving dance and performance workshops. Through sharing their culture, Indigenous Australians are helping other people to understand their way of life.

# ORNAMENT

Art and decoration are central to Indigenous Australian cultures, from painting on wood and rock carving, to ceremonial clothes and body painting. Indigenous Australian art shows Dreamtime stories, daily life, ceremonies, and spirit ancestors, as well as environmental change and historic events.

## Dot paintings

The exact meaning of dot paintings is usually only known by **clan** members. Many of these paintings are sold to tourists and collectors. Important art galleries such as the National Art Gallery in Sydney have collections of Indigenous Australian art on display. One of the most famous dot painters was Clifford Possum Tjapaltjarri (1932–2002). His work was inspired by stories from the Dreamtime.

This dot painting on wood shows many different animals and shapes.

## Emily Kame Kngwarreye (1910–1996)

Emily Kame Kngwarreye was nearly 80 when she started painting seriously. She often painted **yams**, an important source of food for her nation, who live in the Northern Territory. Her paintings won her international fame and are now very valuable.

Paintings like these are often sold for millions of pounds.

## Sand painting

Sand paintings are made as clans move from place to place. The paintings use whatever materials can be found in the environment, such as seeds, flowers, sand, and stones. **Symbols** represent the clan's history and creation story. They also show the location of sacred sites, food sources, and water holes.

## YOUNG PEOPLE

Art was one of the main ways that younger Indigenous Australians learned about their cultures. Elders would sing as they painted, passing on their knowledge to younger clan members.

## Rock art

One of the most important and oldest forms of Indigenous Australian art is rock painting. Paintings found in Koonalda Cave on the Nullarbor Plain have been dated to 20,000 years ago, whilst others in the Olary region of South Australia are estimated to be 40,000 years old.

This rock painting was found in Kakadu National Park in the Northern Territory.

Other rock paintings, however, are relatively recent and are part of a living tradition. They are still very important to people who know and respect their meanings. Indigenous artists use traditional materials to create their interpretations of the landscape, sacred places, and spirit ancestors. A few are even repainted by Indigenous Australian men and women who have the traditional right to do so.

## Did you know?

The soil of Australia contains a clay called ochre. Ochre can make different shades of yellow, brown, and red. These colours are traded between different clans, just like buying paint from a shop.

Indigenous Australians who live in the **outback** still mix ochre powder with water to make paint. Brushes are made from sticks, feathers, grasses, and palm leaves.

## Types of painting

Hunting, ancestral beings, and spirits are all popular images in Indigenous Australian rock paintings. At Split Rock, near Laura, Queensland, there are rock paintings of the spirits Quinkan and Anurra.

In Victoria, the Koorie people painted dozens of children's handprints at Gulgurn Manja (also known as Flat Rock). Some Indigenous Australians believe that the spirit ancestors themselves painted the rock art images.

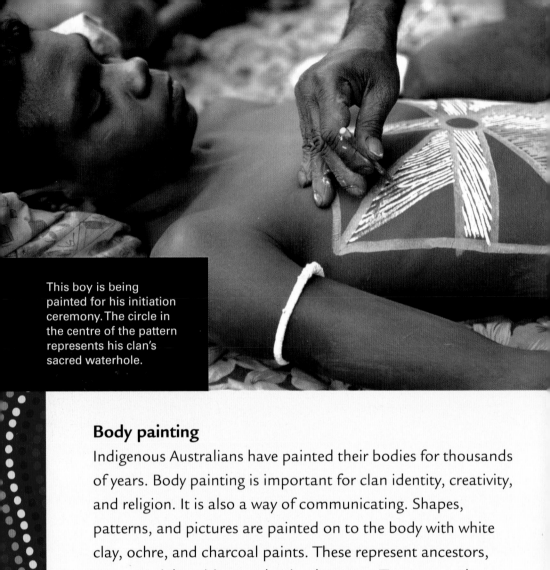

This boy is being painted for his initiation ceremony. The circle in the centre of the pattern represents his clan's sacred waterhole.

## Body painting

Indigenous Australians have painted their bodies for thousands of years. Body painting is important for clan identity, creativity, and religion. It is also a way of communicating. Shapes, patterns, and pictures are painted on to the body with white clay, ochre, and charcoal paints. These represent ancestors, age or social position, and animal **totems**. Totems are also carved on to wood or shell pendants and worn around the neck for special occasions.

## Masks

Indigenous Australians who live in the Torres Strait made masks of birds and sea creatures from wood or turtle shells. These were to ensure success in hunting and for ceremonies and initiations. Today, Torres Strait artists such as Ricardo Idagi are trying to bring back mask-making as an important cultural tradition and link to the past.

## YOUNG PEOPLE

In many Indigenous Australian clans, individuals are given personal totems at birth. Sometimes a person does not eat the animal that their totem represents. This is a mark of respect. For example, they will not eat kangaroo if that is their totem. At large gatherings, young people can identify who is part of their wider community and nation by the totem worn.

Turtleshell masks like this one were often used by the Torres Strait Islander people.

## Did you know?

The Yolngu people of Arnhem Land and the Tiwi people on Bathurst and Melville Islands still paint their bodies for funerals.

## Clothing and religion

Similar to many other people around the world living in hot regions, some Indigenous Australian people traditionally did not wear clothes. They would, however, dress up for ceremonies, **rituals**, and clan gatherings.

Each different nation group had their own types of ceremonial dress. This helped them to connect with their spirit ancestors. Men and women wore different decorations including headgear, necklaces, bracelets, and armbands. Women often wore skirts made from emu or other bird feathers. All these special clothes and decorations were made from things found naturally, such as shells and animal skins.

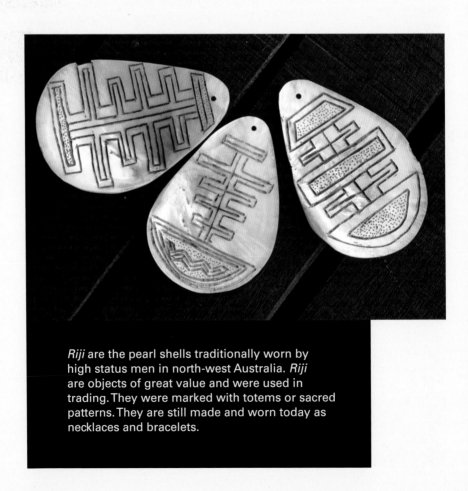

*Riji* are the pearl shells traditionally worn by high status men in north-west Australia. *Riji* are objects of great value and were used in trading. They were marked with totems or sacred patterns. They are still made and worn today as necklaces and bracelets.

## Lenore Dembski (born 1955)

Lenore Dembski is an Indigenous Australian fashion designer. She is called the Paperbark Woman after her people, the Kungarakan, who are known as the Paperbark people. Her designs are influenced by her culture but she works with modern materials. Lenore uses her work to raise awareness of Indigenous Australian culture.

## Animal cloaks

Possum-skin cloaks were made and worn by Indigenous Australians in south-east Australia. The cloaks were made from possum skins sewn together with kangaroo **sinew**. They were often decorated with important clan symbols. They were rubbed with ochre and fat to both decorate and protect them.

Possum-skin cloaks were handed down through generations.

# FAMILY AND SOCIETY

Today, most Indigenous Australians live in modern houses in urban areas. About one-quarter of the population lives in more remote, rural areas. Traditionally, clans numbered about 50 people, but today many young people leave to seek work in larger towns and cities.

## Did you know?

In Australia's outback, the hot sun, heavy rainfall, and strong winds can make life very hard. There are also many harmful animals and insects. Shelters were built according to the protection people needed. Shelters included hollowed-out tree trunks, bark shelters, windbreakers, round huts, and sleeping platforms. A bark shelter is a simple construction that looks like a modern tent.

## Protected areas

Indigenous Australians believe they are **custodians** of the land. They also believe that humans, animals, and spirits are joined together, so they used to stay where their ancestors were. When Europeans arrived in the 18th century, they did not understand this special connection to the land. They took over land that was rich in **resources** and drove the indigenous people away from their homes.

Today, the government has apologized for past wrongs and some Indigenous Australian homelands have been returned. Areas such as Arnhem Land are protected. Non-indigenous people cannot enter these areas without a special pass or invitation.

Some Indigenous Australians live as their ancestors did in places like Arnhem Land. They hunt and fish as their people have done for centuries.

## YOUNG PEOPLE

Today, the Australian government encourages cultural exchange and understanding between white Australians and Indigenous Australians. Indigenous groups in rural and urban areas share their culture with school children. The pupils learn about traditional arts, crafts, and ways of life.

## Daily life

In an Indigenous Australian nation, elders are highly respected. The Wiradjuri people use the word *bidga* to describe the leader of a group, while other nations do not have a particular leader. Every member of a clan has different responsibilities and roles depending on factors such as age, knowledge, and interests. Traditionally, women were responsible for bringing up children and gathering food, while men were responsible for hunting. In most nations, men and women shared the roles of healers, law-makers, and keepers of traditional knowledge.

## Tools and weapons

Men and boys made tools and weapons from things found in the natural environment. Weapons such as spears and clubs were made from stone, shells, wood, and animal bones.

These Tjapukapai men are making a fire.

## YOUNG PEOPLE

At around six years of age, male children traditionally joined the men to learn about hunting large animals such as emu and kangaroo. Young girls remained with the women to learn about food gathering. The girls were taught which nuts, berries, and roots to collect.

## Fibrecraft

The women of Peppimenarti and Oenpelli are famous for their weaving, but every community has its own styles and techniques. Baskets were often made from twisted tree bark fibres. Kurrajong, river wattle, banyan, and peanut trees were commonly used barks. Other weaving fibres were made from a mixture of grasses and human hair. Bags, wall hangings, floor mats, and fishing nets were all woven.

Traditional crafts such as weaving are still practised today. Some of the products are sold to tourists.

## Food and hunting

Indigenous Australians were traditionally hunter-gatherers. They moved around the country either on foot or in canoes to search for food. They knew how to track their environment and read the different signs that signalled the seasons, such as **locusts** swarming. When they found food, they communicated with other groups using a bullroarer. This is a flat piece of wood on a string, which makes a whirring noise when it is spun. The noise can be heard over long distances.

Men used weapons such as *woomera* (spears) and boomerangs when hunting for food.

## YOUNG PEOPLE

Traditionally, as soon as children can walk, they learn to track their mother's and sibling's footprints. They also learn to recognize animal tracks. By learning young, the children become experts in tracking and are able to tell how big an animal is, whether it is male or female, and even which way a snake is travelling!

## Bushtucker

Food which is found in the wild is called bushtucker in Australia. Some Indigenous Australians still track and gather their food from the bush. Insects, snakes, lizards, honey ants, and witchetty grubs are all healthy foods. Nations who live near the coast eat shellfish, lobster, crab, and mussels.

Tasty witchetty grubs are found in the roots of the witchetty bush.

## Did you know?

The names of some native Australian animals have come from Indigenous Australian languages. *Koala, kangaroo, wombat, wallaby, barramundi, budgerigar,* and *kookaburra* are all indigenous words that have entered the English language.

# PERFORMANCE

Among the most spectacular shows of Indigenous Australian culture are the colourful dances that are regularly performed in the outback. Different communities come together for a few days of music, dance, and celebration. Traditionally, neighbouring clans were invited to gatherings by message sticks. These are an ancient form of written communication. Message sticks are solid pieces of wood around 30 centimetres (12 inches) long, and are marked with lines and dots.

## Did you know?

The peoples of central Australia call social gatherings *purlapa*. At a *purlapa*, a stamping dance is usually performed by men and boys. The dancers paint their bodies and decorate themselves with *wamurlu*, a kind of wild cotton.

At the Garma Festival in Arnhem Land, indigenous people wear special clothes and body paint for performances.

## Dance

The Garma Festival takes place each year in Arnhem Land, whilst the Barunga Festival takes place in the Northern Territory. Probably the best-known festival is the Laura Dance Festival in Queensland. The Bangarra Dance Theatre performs spectacular modern dance shows all over the world inspired by the dancers' culture.

Dancing styles vary between nations. In some dances, performers are transformed into the spirit ancestor they are portraying. Typically, men jump and stamp their feet while women clap and chant. Some dances mimic (copy) animals or birds. Each dance has a song and is usually accompanied by clapping sticks and the didgeridoo.

### Sean Choolburra

Sean Choolburra is a well-known Indigenous Australian comedian and cultural performer. He visits schools all over the world and leads cultural workshops. He has even been known to play hip-hop on the didgeridoo!

## Making music

Indigenous Australians believe the world was sung into existence by the spirit ancestors during the Dreamtime. Music and song are at the heart of their culture. Gatherings such as the Gattjirrk music festival on Milingimbi Island celebrate different clans' musical traditions. Each clan has its own storytelling songs called *bunggul*.

### Geoffrey Gurrumul Yunupingu (born 1970)

Geoffrey Gurrumul Yunupingu is a famous blind Indigenous Australian musician. He only speaks a few words of English, and records in the Yolngu language. He sings about the stories of his Gumatj clan.

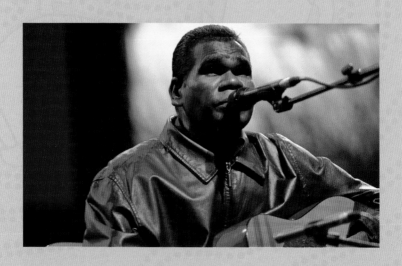

## Musical instruments

Traditional Indigenous Australian music consists of **rhythmic** singing and percussion-style instruments. Handclaps, body slapping, and *blima* (clapsticks) keep the beat going. Drums are made out of lizard skin and rattles are made from bunches of seed pods.

The didgeridoo is an ancient wind instrument. Still made and played today, it is are made from branches of stringybark, woollybark, or bloodwood trees that have been hollowed out by **termites**. The sound is produced by blowing and buzzing down the hollow wooden tube.

Didgeridoos are believed to have been first made in Arnhem Land 2,000 years ago.

## Did you know?

Traditionally, didgeridoos are only played by men. Today, anyone can play them, but not during ceremonies and sacred rituals.

Today, Indigenous Australian music is a mixture of traditional and modern instruments and modern pop and hip-hop beats. Country music is also popular. Musicians, such as the group Yothu Yindi and singers Archie Roach and Christine Anu, use their lyrics to protest about politics, raise environmental awareness, and to celebrate their culture.

## Film and television

In the last 30 years, Indigenous Australian actors, playwrights, and filmmakers have starred in popular television programmes, won major awards, and been inspired by their culture and history to produce important documentaries and films. National Indigenous Television broadcasts news and cultural programmes across Australia.

### Deborah Mailman (born 1972)

Deborah Mailman was the first Indigenous Australian actor to win the Australian Film Institute Award. She won Best Actress in a Leading Role for *Radiance* (1998). She has also filmed a documentary called *Going Bush* with athlete Cathy Freeman, about different indigenous groups and their culture.

## Film festival

In 1999, the first Message Sticks Indigenous Film Festival took place. The festival tours Australia and all the films are free. Allan Collins, Danielle Maclean, Darlene Johnson, and John Macumba are all well-known Indigenous Australian filmmakers.

## Theatre performance

Each June, the Festival of the Dreaming takes place in Woodford, Queensland. Plays written by Indigenous Australian writers are performed. The plays might be about Dreaming stories, the past, comedy tales, or the historical wrongs against indigenous people.

# Did you know?

One of the most successful Australian films of all time is *Rabbit-Proof Fence* (2002). Based on a book by Doris Pilkington Garimara, called *Follow the Rabbit-Proof Fence*, the film deals with the Stolen Generations, a very important part of Australian history.

Between 1869 and 1970, Indigenous Australian children were forcibly removed from their families by the Australian Government. They were taken away to be trained as servants at government institutions, and were often treated very badly. They lost touch with their families and cultures. In 2008, the Australian Government apologized for the grief and suffering this policy had caused.

The film *Rabbit-Proof Fence* won awards around the world.

# CUSTOMS AND ACTIVITIES

Many traditional **customs** and games prepared young Indigenous Australian children for hunting and survival. For example, *battendi* was a spear-throwing game, and *bubberah* involved boomerang throwing. *Goomboobooddoo* is a traditional wrestling game and *kee'an* involved throwing an animal bone with twine attached to it into a hole.

Today, sports and games are still important to Indigenous Australians. Some indigenous athletes, such as Benn Harradine, Otis Gowa, and Nathan Jawai, have competed at the highest levels in international sports events such as the Olympic Games.

## Cathy Freeman (born 1973)

Cathy Freeman is a champion 400-metre runner who won gold at the 2000 Sydney Olympics. After retiring in 2003, she set up her own foundation, which promotes sport and healthy lifestyle projects with young Indigenous Australians.

## Woggabaliri

*Woggabaliri* is a team game played with a ball made of possum skin. It is played mainly by the Wiradjuri people of New South Wales. The ball is kicked and volleyed as in football. The Djab wurrung and Jardwadjali peoples played a game called *marn grook*, possibly the inspiration for Australian Rules Football.

### Did you know?

The annual Aboriginal Rugby League Carnival in New South Wales is the biggest senior rugby league competition in the world. Up to 70 teams and their supporters come together for one weekend to represent their communities.

## Barunga festival

The annual Barunga sports and cultural festival is organized by the Jawoyn people in the Northern Territory. Indigenous and other Australian people gather, take part in team sports, and watch traditional and modern dances.

Spear-throwing contests are among the activities held at the Barunga sports and cultural festival.

## Health and healing

Indigenous Australians have always made their own medicine from the plants and animals in their environment. Known as "bush medicine", these natural cures are still used today by some communities.

Traditional healers – both men and women – are known as *ngangkari*. Warlpiri women still perform *yawylyu* ceremonies to help people who are ill. They sing and paint healing pictures on the ill person.

## Did you know?

When Europeans arrived in Australia in 1788, they brought new diseases that Indigenous Australians had no **immunity** against. In 1789, a smallpox epidemic in Sydney wiped out around 50 per cent of the local indigenous population. Today, Indigenous Australians have a life expectancy of 17 years less than the Australian average. This is because of poverty and a lack of equal opportunities, issues that many people are fighting to address.

Emus are large flightless birds found only in Australia. Indigenous Australians traditionally used emu fat to make oil for treating burns, wounds, and arthritis.

## How medicines are made and used

Bush medicines are made from mixing berries, seeds, and leaves with animal fats. Plants are often ground and boiled before being mixed with fat to make ointments. This can be used on rashes, burns, or stings. Leaves are boiled in water to make a kind of tea that is drunk or applied to cuts to prevent infection. Honey is also used to clean wounds. For chest infections, leaves are put on a fire and the smoke is inhaled.

Modern medicine is easy to obtain but some clans are trying hard to keep their traditional healing knowledge. Here, healers Djerrkngu Marika (left) and Bablangua Manungurr are preparing a fire for bush medicines.

## Writers and story-tellers

Dreaming stories have been handed down from generation to generation over thousands of years. These stories are still passed on **orally**, although many are now recorded in print and on film.

Indigenous Australian children learn about Dreaming stories from a very early age. Clan elders tell them stories to help them understand the land, the universe, their culture, and their people. When the children become adults, they become the storytellers for the next generation.

This Indigenous Australian family live in Arnhem Land. They will pass their culture on from generation to generation, as has been done for centuries.

## Did you know?

The *Koori Mail* newspaper is written and owned by Indigenous Australian people. Published every two weeks, it is read by over 90,000 people across Australia. The *Koori Mail* website is also accessed by many people around the world.

## Book culture

Over the last century, Indigenous Australian writers have written about their own culture. Through their work, they have brought greater understanding and awareness of indigenous issues to other people.

In 1964, Oodgeroo Noonuccal (1920–1993) published the first Indigenous Australian poetry collection, *We Are Going.* In 1987, Sally Morgan published her life story, *My Place*, which brought indigenous culture to a wider audience. The plays of Jack Davis are studied in schools across Australia.

### David Unaipon (1872–1967)

David Unaipon was a member of the Ngarrindjeri people. He was a writer, a preacher, an artist, and an inventor. He wrote traditional indigenous stories and he was the first indigenous writer to be published. His picture appears on the AUS$50 note.

Oodgeroo Noonuccal's name used to be Kath Walker. She changed it to make it clear she was Oodgeroo of the Noonuccal tribe.

# INDIGENOUS AUSTRALIAN CULTURES IN THE 21ST CENTURY

In the past, Indigenous Australian cultures were usually described and presented by non-indigenous people. This led to many inaccurate and contradictory ideas of what Indigenous Australian cultures were like.

Today, organizations such as the Australian Institute for Aboriginal and Torres Strait Islander Studies are helping indigenous people to change how they are represented. By collecting stories, photos, films, and recording interviews with Indigenous Australians from many different nation groups, researchers are building and presenting a more accurate picture of indigenous cultures.

## Did you know?

Governments of the past have not always listened and responded to the needs of Indigenous Australian people. Many people, both indigenous and non-indigenous, have fought long and hard to change this.

In 2010, the Australian government announced plans to change the country's **constitution** to recognize Indigenous Australians. All Australians will vote on whether to make this change.

There are also plans for new policies and reforms to improve education, health, jobs, and housing for Indigenous Australians.

Indigenous Australians have a long history to be proud of, and a bright future to work towards.

## One country, three flags

The Indigenous Australian flag and the Torres Strait Islander flags are two of the official flags of Australia. The Indigenous Australian flag was designed in 1971 by indigenous artist Harold Thomas. It contains a black strip, a yellow circle in the centre, and a red strip. The black represents the Indigenous Australian people, the red represents Earth, and the yellow represents the Sun.

## Modern culture

Today, Indigenous Australian people contribute to all aspects of Australian society and life. Their cultures have had to adapt to the changes brought by European invasion. With strong faith systems, these cultures are using their creativity to spread understanding and to survive.

# TIMELINE

BCE

*c.* 50,000    Indigenous Australians arrive in Australia and the Torres Strait Islands

*c.* 20,000    Cave paintings are made at Koonalda Cave

CE

1st century    The didgeridoo is invented

1788    Europeans arrive to settle in Australia

1869    The Stolen Generations policy begins

1938    The 150th anniversary of the European invasion, a day of mourning for Indigenous Australians

1967    Indigenous Australians gain formal recognition of their existence as citizens of their country

1971    Harold Thomas designs the Indigenous Australian flag

1993    The first Laura Dance Festival is held

2000    Cathy Freeman lights the Olympic Torch at the Sydney Games and wins 400-metre gold

2001    Carol Martin becomes the first Indigenous Australian woman to be voted into parliament

2002    *Rabbit Proof Fence* wins awards around the world

2007    *Warlugulong*, a painting by Clifford Possum Tjapaltjarri, sells for AUS$2.4 million (£1.02 million)

2007    National Indigenous Television begins broadcasting

2008    Prime Minister Kevin Rudd formally apologizes to the Stolen Generation

# CULTURAL MAP

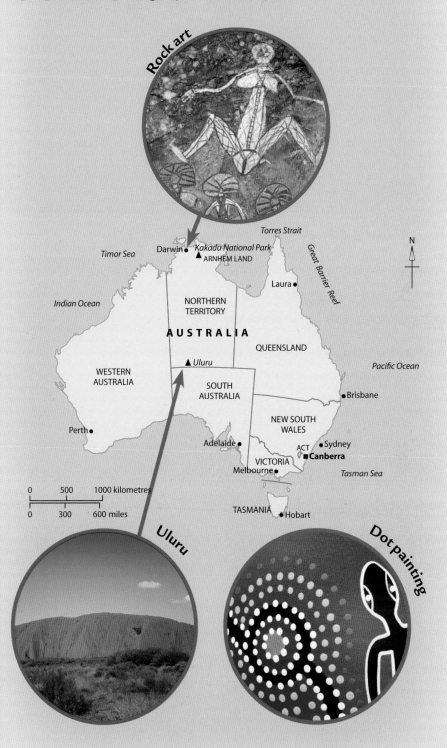

Rock art

Torres Strait

Timor Sea

Darwin •  *Kakadu National Park*
▲ ARNHEM LAND

Great Barrier Reef

Laura •

N

Indian Ocean

NORTHERN
TERRITORY

**AUSTRALIA**

QUEENSLAND

Pacific Ocean

▲ *Uluru*

WESTERN
AUSTRALIA

SOUTH
AUSTRALIA

• Brisbane

NEW SOUTH
WALES

Perth •

Adelaide •

ACT  • Sydney
■ **Canberra**

VICTORIA
Melbourne •

Tasman Sea

| 0 | 500 | 1000 kilometres |
|---|-----|-----------------|
| 0 | 300 | 600 miles |

TASMANIA
• Hobart

Uluru

Dot painting

# GLOSSARY

**ancestor** family relation from a very long time ago, such as a great-great-grandparent

**clan** group of families or villages that share a common culture

**constitution** legal document which outlines the basic laws of a country

**creation story** story that describes how a people were created, how the world began, and how they came into it

**culture** customs, social organisation, and achievements of a particular nation, people, or group

**custodian** person responsible for looking after something valuable

**custom** way things have been done for a long time

**didgeridoo** traditional Indigenous Australian wind instrument

**elder** senior member of a family or clan

**folklore** traditional local stories passed down in a community

**heritage** anything from the past handed down by tradition

**immunity** resistance to disease

**indigenous** original inhabitants of a certain place or region

**initiation** ceremony or test to mark someone joining a group

**locust** large species of grasshopper. Locusts travel in huge swarms, eating all the vegetation in their path.

**oral** spoken

**outback** remote inland area, with a low population

**resource** natural supplies of a country such as wood, gold, oil, and minerals

**rhythmic** with a strong beat or rhythm

**rite of passage** important process that marks the beginning of a new part of one's life

**ritual** formal actions in a ceremony

**sinew** part of the body that attaches a muscle to a bone

**symbol** sign

**termite** insect similar to an ant, that lives in large groups called colonies

**totem** object or thing in nature that is adopted as a family emblem

**tradition** customs that are passed on from one generation to the next

**yam** root of a climbing vine found in tropical countries

# FIND OUT MORE

## Books

*Australia (Countries Around the World)*, Mary Colson
  (Raintree, 2011)

*Kakadu Calling: Stories for Kids*, Jane Garlil Christophersen
  (Magabala Books, 2007)

*Stories from the Billabong*, James Vance Marshall and Francis
  Firebrace (Frances Lincoln Children's Books, 2010)

*Australian Aborigines (People Under Threat)*, Richard Nile
  (Wayland, 2010)

## Websites

**www.aiatsis.gov.au**
Visit the website of the Australian Institute for Aboriginal and
Torres Strait Islander Studies.

**australianmuseum.net.au/Indigenous-Australia**
Learn more about topics related to Indigenous Australians,
including spirituality, cultural heritage, the land, and more.

**burarra.questacon.edu.au/home.html**
Meet Danaja and his grandfather, Wala Wala, and find out
about life in an Indigenous Australian community.

**www.nla.gov.au/exhibitions/bunyips**
Are you scared of *bunyips*? If you dare, check out the National
Library of Australia's website for stories, games, and quizzes.

## CDs and DVDs

*The Rough Guide to Australian Aboriginal Music* (World Music
  Network, 2008)

*Rabbit-Proof Fence* (2002)

## Places to visit

If you ever get the chance to go to Australia, these are some places you could visit:

**Uluru, Northern Territory**
Visit Australia's most famous rock. Take a guided tour around the sacred sites and see the amazing rock art.

**Kakadu National Park, Northern Territory**
See rock art images of spirit ancestors and hunting in this spectacular landscape.

**Tjapukai Aboriginal Cultural Park, Cairns, Queensland**
Watch theatre and dance performances and learn the traditional ways of the Tjapukai people. Make bush medicines and learn to play the didgeridoo.

**Brambuk National Park and Cultural Centre, Victoria**
This cultural centre is shared between five indigenous communities. Take a bush food tour and try out crocodile and kangaroo in the Bush Café!

## More topics to research

What topic did you like reading about most in this book? Did you find out anything that you thought was particularly interesting? Choose a topic that you liked, such as food, art, or religion, and try to find out more about it. You could have a look at one of the websites or visit your local library to do some research. You could also try some things out for yourself – listen to some Indigenous Australian music, or make a dot painting on tree bark.

# INDEX